The Model T has had a loyal following amongst enthusiasts over the years. A 1923 coachbuilt Landaulette is being flagged off in a 1973 Model T Ford Register rally in London's Pall Mall. The thirty-seven Ts were then driven to the Ford Parts Distribution Centre at Daventry, Northamptonshire.

The Model T Ford

Jonathan Wood

Shire Publications

Contents

Cover: A car for all seasons, as depicted on a British edition of the corporate Ford Times. *This Manchester-assembled right-hand-drive Model T retained its brass radiator for longer than the American version. It switched to a black radiator in August 1916, Trafford Park's transition being May to August 1917. The production figures on the board revealed the car's astounding success. The world total for 1917 was destined to leap to over 750,000, more than three times 1914's figure.*

ACKNOWLEDGEMENTS

My grateful thanks to Ford historian David Burgess-Wise and Bruce Lilleker, chairman of the Model T Ford Register, for their help in the preparation of this Album. Most of the photographs and the cover picture are reproduced by courtesy of the Ford Motor Company and I am grateful to John Moulton for the loan of the picture on page 19 (bottom). The remainder are from the author's collection.

British Library Cataloguing in Publication Data: Wood, Jonathan. The Model T Ford. – (Shire album; no. 348) 1. Ford Model T automobile – History I. Title 629.2'222 ISBN 0 7478 0432 X

Editorial Consultant: Michael E. Ware, Director of the National Motor Museum, Beaulieu.

Published in 2008 by Shire Publications Ltd, Midland House, West Way, Botley, Oxford OX2 0PH, UK (Website: www.shirebooks.co.uk)
Copyright © 1999 by Jonathan Wood. Published in 1999 and 2008. Shire Album 348. ISBN 978 0 74780 432 1. Jonathan Wood is hereby identified as the author of this work in accordance with Section 77 of the Copyright, Designs and Patents Act 1988.

Printed in Great Britain by Ashford Colour Press Ltd, Unit 600, Fareham Reach, Fareham Road, Gosport, Hampshire PO13 0FW.

A self-taught genius

Today, with the world's highways playing host to some seventy different makes of car, it is almost impossible to comprehend the impact of the Model T Ford. Introduced in 1908 and mass-produced from 1914, incredibly by 1921 half the motor cars on the road were 'Tin Lizzies' (as the Model T became popularly known). With over sixteen and a half million produced, it was, until overtaken by the Volkswagen Beetle in 1973, the most popular car in the history of the automobile.

But the T also taught the motor industry how to manufacture its cars and Ford methods of assembly were destined to endure until the 1980s, when they were supplanted by Japan's lean production techniques. In corporate terms, the Model T consolidated the Ford Motor Company's position as a leading car maker. It was the USA's (and thus the world's) largest motor manufacturer between 1906 and 1926, and its founder, Henry Ford (1863–1947), became an American folk hero.

In the best traditions of the breed, he was born in a substantial but unpretentious wooden house that his father had built with his own hands. Irish-born William Ford was a farmer with land at Dearborn near the city of Detroit, Michigan, and Henry was the first of six children. After attending the local Scotch Settlement School,

which he left at the age of twelve, he received no further formal education. Ford possessed, however, an unalloyed bent for mechanical matters that flowered into a kind of genius. He delighted in tinkering with and repairing watches, and in 1871 he left the farm to work in a Detroit machine shop. It was to lead him to produce his first experimental car in 1896, a single-cylinder Quadricycle, and in 1899 the Detroit Automobile Company was established to manufacture it. This proved to be a short-lived venture, as did the Henry Ford Company that succeeded it.

At the age of thirty-nine, Ford was luckier on his third attempt, and the Ford Motor Company was formed on 16th June 1903. Premises were established in an old, close-boarded wagon shop in Mack Avenue, Detroit, and, in July, a Dr Pfennig placed an order

By 1917 the Model T was well on its way to becoming a world car as these right-hand-drive examples featured on the cover of the British edition of the 'Ford Times' indicate.

for one of the company's first cars, designated the Model A. Henry Ford was on his way.

The Model A was a cheap and simple two-cylinder 8 hp car. It was soon followed, in 1904, by the first four-cylinder Ford, the 4.6 litre Model B, which paved the way in 1906 for another four, the 2.5 litre N two-seater Runabout, the forerunner of the Model T. The 8729 cars produced that year made Ford the United States' largest car maker. The company had moved, early in 1905, to a purpose-designed three-storey brick factory on the corner of the city's Beaubien and Piquette Avenues.

It was there that the N's successor was planned. In 1907 came the R, a de luxe N and the S, a combination of both types that was also available in four-seater form, so the next available letter in the corporate alphabet was T.

The motivation for the new car was Henry Ford's belief in the potential of light, strong vanadium steel, which also had the virtue of being shock-resistant. It had been pioneered by the French but improved in Britain between 1899 and 1902. Ford's interest dated from 1905; he first used it on the Model N and is credited with introducing the alloy to the American motor industry. In order to reap the full benefits of the material, Ford envisaged a completely new car in which the triple qualities of lightness, power and durability were paramount.

Work on the project began in 1906 and, although a dozen or so individuals were concerned with its creation, there were four key players at the apex of the design process. At their head was Henry Ford himself. He was ably assisted by Childe Harold Wills, who made a speciality of metallurgy and had joined the company in 1902. A more recent recruit was Hungarian engineer Joseph Galamb, who arrived in 1905, whilst Ed 'Spider' Huff had been with Ford since the 1890s. They occupied a small room on the third floor of the factory containing a blackboard on which Ford

4

One of the cars that predated the T, the two-cylinder Model F of 1905–6. The London-based Central Motor Car Company was formed in November 1904 although Ford imports to Britain had begun earlier, over the winter of 1903–4.

THE FORD CAR.

MODEL F. 14 Brake Horse Power.

Price as Illustrated with Side Entrance Tonneau,

£275.

Price as Illustrated with Side Entrance Tonneau,

£275.

SPECIFICATION.

Weight	1,400 pounds.
Motor	Ford 2 Cylinder, horizontal opposed 4½ × 4.
Wheelbase	84 inches.
Wheels	30 inches.
Tyres	3½ inch Continental.
Maximum Speed	35 miles an hour.
Petrol Tank Capacity	9 gallons.

Colour: Dark Green, Yellow Running Gear.
Upholstering: Black Leather.

<u>Reliable & Stylish.</u>   <u>Simple & Economical.</u>

FORD
SHOWROOMS.
The Central Motor Car Company, Ltd.,
117, LONG ACRE, W.C.

Telegrams:
"AMMOTICAR," LONDON.

Nat. Telephones:
5011 GERRARD.
3137 do.

jotted down his thoughts. These would then be interpreted by Galamb and his team. Sitting in his mother's rocking chair in the corner, Henry Ford talked far into the night about the car that was to bring motoring to the multitude.

Next door was a larger room, big enough to take a chassis, all-important drilling and milling machines and a lathe. It was here that the car took shape.

The work took some two years to complete and was finalised by the beginning of 1908. An advance catalogue was issued on 18th March and six months later Ford's branch managers were summoned to Detroit to hear full details of the car. In the meantime work was proceeding apace on the design, and an unnumbered pre-production car was completed on 24th September 1908. (Model T number one was finished three days later, on 27th September.)

On its completion, Ford, accompanied by two colleagues, then took the prototype tourer on a 1357 mile (2183 km) hunting trip to northern Wisconsin. It averaged 20 mph (32 km/h) and performed with great reliability, a pertinent pointer to the future. By the time the party returned to Detroit on 2nd October, the new Ford had been officially announced for the 1909 season, although there was no opportunity for the American public to examine Ford's new car properly until the New York Automobile Show, which opened on 31st December.

Henry Ford clearly looked upon the Model T as a vehicle that could be sold throughout the world and the first eight examples built were shipped to Europe. The car's first public display was in London, at the Motor Show held at Olympia on 13th November, followed by the Paris event later the same month. In the latter exhibition, apart from Buick, the Ford was the only American car on show. With an encouraging response from dealers and public, the omens looked good.

Although this photograph of a British-built 1913 right-hand-drive car has suffered the ravages of time, it clearly shows the ingenuity of the Model T's chassis and mechanicals. Note the high ground clearance and front and rear radius arms.

The mass-produced masterpiece

It would be misleading to suggest that the Model T was, on its announcement, a particularly cheap car. The open-bodied version sold for $850 (£175), $100 (£20) more than the well-equipped R. So if it was not the price that attracted potential buyers, what did make this outwardly orthodox Ford so special?

With a 100 inch (2540 mm) wheelbase, the T was initially available with a choice of five open and closed bodies. But it was the five-seater Touring Car, appealing to the family man, that was the most popular line and was destined to remain so throughout the model's nineteen-year production life. Equally enduring was the two-seater Runabout but the closed versions (the Town Car, the Landaulette and the Coupé) sold in much smaller numbers.

The same chassis was used for all these bodies. It was a simple channel-section frame, easy to manufacture with straight side members and relatively narrow in comparison to its length. As on the Model N, the front suspension was by a single transverse-leaf spring although the N's rear half-elliptics were dispensed with and the transverse design repeated. Both springs were made of vanadium steel. The price of two springs was saved as a result although the arrangement required the use of twin radius rods fore and aft. Ford made great play of his triangulated 'three-point suspension', which was also repeated in the three-point engine mounting. All helped to isolate the flexible chassis from the worst of the world's roads.

With wood in plentiful supply, the Model T, like so many of its contemporaries, was fitted with hickory-spoked wheels, of 30 inches (762 mm) diameter. Significantly, the car cleared the highway by a substantial 10.5 inches (267 mm) and was able to cope with the American roads of the day, which were often deeply rutted, with such metalling as there was often swept away by the winter rains.

Another British-built right-hand-drive car, dating from 1912, which shows Ford's three-point transverse-leaf front suspension. The apparently fragile but immensely strong vanadium steel front axle is clearly visible.

The location of the steering wheel differed from Ford's earlier models, and indeed practically all American cars, because it was positioned on the left. Hitherto, American manufacturers had aped European practice and mounted the steering gear on the right, even though Americans drove on the right. But left-hand steering was, said the company, the 'logical side for American roads' and the rest of the industry soon followed the T's example.

To European eyes the Ford's chassis appeared extraordinarily fragile, yet it was as tough and enduring as Henry Ford himself. This is because many of the key components, such as the drop-forged front axle and transmission parts, were also made from vanadium steel.

Three-point mounting was also applied to the engine and rear suspension. The torque tube transmission was wholly enclosed.

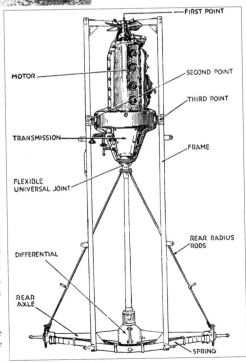

FIRST POINT

MOTOR

SECOND POINT

THIRD POINT

TRANSMISSION

FRAME

FLEXIBLE UNIVERSAL JOINT

REAR RADIUS RODS

DIFFERENTIAL

REAR AXLE

SPRING

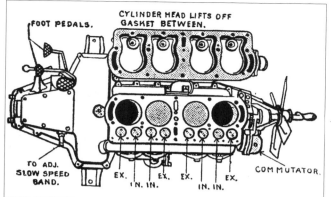

The Model T's engine of 1908 was innovative in featuring a detachable cylinder head. Its transmission was also mounted in unit with the power unit, rather than being separated from it.

If the T's frame was a traditional, cost-conscious design, behind the handsome brass radiator was a 176.7 cubic inch (2895 cc) four-cylinder side-valve engine that bristled with innovation and ingenuity. Like so many of its contemporaries, Ford's Model N had been powered by a similarly configured power unit that consisted of a pair of cast-iron fixed head blocks that each contained two cylinders. These were mounted on an aluminium crankcase. However, the T differed radically from this, and from most other engines of its day for that matter. Not only were the four cylinders produced as a single casting but this was also extended to form the crankcase. In an orthodox fixed-head engine, this design would make the combustion chambers virtually inaccessible. So Ford flew in the face of convention and, despite fears of leakage, made it detachable. Such was the Model T's impact that within thirty years all of these features were to be found in almost every mass-produced car engine. They still are.

At the other end of the power unit, the tough but spindly three-bearing crankshaft was also made of vanadium steel, as were the connecting rods and gears for the side-located camshaft.

A further tilt at convention was the fitment of an archaic but durable ignition system. This took the form of a low-tension flywheel magneto which provided power, via four trembler coils, to the spark plugs. This was the contribution of

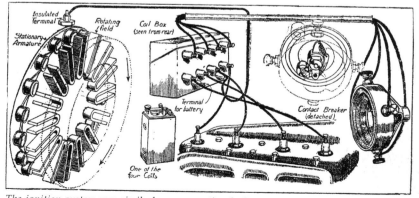

The ignition system was similarly unconventional. Current was supplied by a low-tension flywheel magneto via four trembler coils mounted on the driving compartment side of the bulkhead, where they remained until 1926. They were then repositioned under the bonnet on the left of the engine.

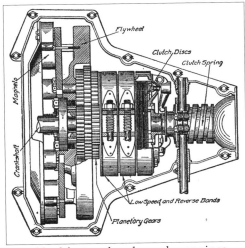

The two-speed epicyclic gearbox. Because of the presence of the magneto, one of the box's more unusual features is that the clutch is located behind the gear train rather than being positioned between the flywheel and gearbox. Unlike its exposed Model N predecessor, it was lubricated by engine oil.

'Spider' Huff, who had grown up in England, and the magneto was probably inspired by the ingenious Birmingham-built Lanchester.

The essence of the T's two-speed gearbox was also rooted in the formidable and creative mind of Frederick Lanchester. His epicyclic train, actuated by contracting brake bands, is still at the heart of most modern automatic transmission systems and was popular in many early American cars as it considerably eased gear-changing. Ford had featured such gearboxes since he started building cars in 1903 and the design of the T's gearbox was carried over, in essence, from the Model N. But it differed significantly in two respects: it was enclosed, and, instead of the N's lever, changes were effected by three pedals. The right-hand pedal applied the car's transmission brake, the central one was de-

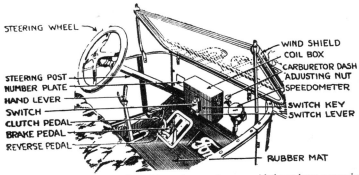

The Ford's three pedal controls: a simple and ingenious system, provided you have never driven before!

pressed to engage reverse gear whilst the left-hand one effected the two speeds and neutral, low being actuated when pushed to the floor, high when released. Engine revolutions were controlled by a hand throttle mounted on the right of the steering column whilst the one on the left operated the ignition advance/retard.

There was more to the hand-brake lever than met the eye because its initial application engaged the left-hand pedal's neutral position. Further down its travel, it applied the brakes, although only, as befitted the day, to the back wheels. In the original design there were two

Starting a recalcitrant Model T involved chocking the front wheels, whilst the rear axle differential meant that it was necessary to jack up only one of the back ones.

levers, the second being used to engage reverse gear. However, after about eight hundred Ts had been built, this was dispensed with early in 1909 and replaced by the middle pedal.

This was a simple and ingenious system for the first-time motorist. By contrast, today's driver would be nonplussed when, on depressing what appears to be a clutch pedal prior to engaging gear, the car starts to move forward. With the Model T, the motoring lessons of a lifetime have to be unlearnt, as the author can vouch!

Where the T also differed from its contemporaries was that, instead of being separated from the power unit by a short driveshaft, the gearbox was mounted in unit with it, just like on a modern engine. This not only saved weight, the cost of the driveshaft and a gearbox subframe, but the engine and transmission could be installed in the chassis as a single unit, thus speeding and simplifying the production process.

Because of the rear transverse-leaf spring suspension, power was conveyed to the rear wheels by a torque tube which meant that the entire engine/transmission was completely enclosed. This protected the potentially vulnerable mechanical components from the perils of the road, dust and stones.

Weighing a mere 1200 pounds (544 kg), the T was capable of 45 mph (72km/h), with low gear effective up to about 15 mph (24 km/h). In truth, it was at its happiest at around 30 mph (48 km/h); above that, the limitations of the suspension and steering became more apparent.

The car that put the world on wheels was not without its faults. Cold-weather starting could be a frustrating business. The flywheel-magneto/trembler-coil design was not the most efficient of arrangements and could require many swings of the fixed starting handle. As temperatures plummeted in the winter, oil left on the clutch plates could congeal. This meant that, when the luckless Model T owner came to swing the engine, the sticking clutch ensured that he was effectively trying to turn the back wheels! The answer was to jack up one of them and release the hand-brake. This then allowed the engine/transmission to turn and the Ford would burst into life. Once running, the seemingly unbreakable Tin Lizzie represented excellent value for money, particularly after 1914 when mass production took over.

In 1909, the first full year of Model T production, Ford built a total of 12,448 cars – about double the 1906 figure. Henry Ford clearly had a winner on his hands and, in that first year of manufacture, he once again flew in the face of convention by dropping all his other models to concentrate on the new car. His belief in the success of the T must have been absolute because in 1907, the year prior to its introduction,

Ford's Highland Park factory in 1915. Built around a reinforced concrete skeleton, it fronted Detroit's Woodward Avenue with Manchester Avenue on the right. The building on the extreme right is appropriately named the Motor Quick Lunch Restaurant!

the Ford company had bought a 56 acre (23 hectare) site previously occupied by an old racecourse fronting Woodward Avenue in the Highland Park district of Detroit. There he built the largest car factory the world had ever seen, eventually covering 278 acres (113 hectares). Possessing its own power station and foundry, the complex of four-storey structures was designed by Albert Kahn, a talented German-born, Detroit-based architect.

In January 1910, Ford began to move into the plant, an operation that would not be completed until 1912. But as demand for the T showed no sign of abating, with 34,528 built in 1911, the company began to experience very real problems in coping with this output. The breaking point came in 1911 when one day's production reached 1300 cars. As the company later revealed: 'the ensuing freight car tie-up was one of the worst traffic jams in the history of Michigan railroading.' Since 1909, Ford had introduced a policy of delegating Model T assembly to some local branches but, following the 1911 gridlock, the process was accelerated and by 1913 there were thirty-one Ford assembly facilities scattered throughout the United States. From then on Highland Park only produced sufficient numbers of Model Ts to satisfy the needs of the Detroit branch.

Output leapt again to 168,220 cars produced in 1913. This was a year in which the Ford management team began to examine ways of increasing production by changing the way in which the T was built.

At this time the assembly process was essentially a stationary one. The front and rear axles were laid on the factory floor; the chassis, complete with springs, was then added, to be followed by the remaining chassis parts. The answer was the moving-track assembly line. Ford's Danish production chief, 'Cast Iron Charlie' Sorensen, had experimented with such a system back in 1908 at Piquette Avenue but it had been set aside. Its later adoption, recalled Sorensen, was driven by the fact that in 1913, 'even though we were operating round the clock shifts, production was still behind demand'.

It was against such a background that the Highland Park engineers once again addressed the problem. It cannot be said that Henry Ford invented the mass production process that resulted – some elements already existed in the American rifle, clock and watch, bicycle and sewing machine industries. Mass production would not have been possible without the T's four thousand or so individual mechanical components being interchangeable one with another. Fortunately for Ford, at this time the United States led the world in this exacting discipline and its machine tool industry was well geared to the challenge. All the ingredients of a manufacturing revolution were thus in place when, on or about 1st April 1913, a conveyor-belt system was applied for the first time for the assembly of a Model T component, in this instance its flywheel magneto. When this proved successful, the approach was transferred to the chassis.

Using stationary assembly, the best time attained by the company had been in September 1913, when it had taken 12 hours 28 minutes to build a car. Then over a seven-month period, between October 1913 and April 1914, the principles of the moving-track assembly line were proved and perfected. On 3rd April, a T was assembled in just 1 hour 33 minutes, over ten times faster than the old method. With the Model T, Henry Ford had produced the right car at the right time. He could now build it in the right way.

In 1914, the first full year of the moving track, output soared to 248,307 and the Highland Park workforce was swelled by the introduction, in January, of the $5 (£1.02) wage for an eight-hour working day.

The arrival of the track gave birth to Henry Ford's famous maxim that 'any customer can have a car painted any colour that he wants so long as it is black'.

The moving-track assembly line, Highland Park, 1914. It illustrates the point where the chassis, which had hitherto slid on the rails on the left, now run on their own wheels. In the interests of safety, the chain that drove the line was enclosed within a sheet metal cover.

Hitherto, black had not been listed as a Ford colour although, perversely, some examples do survive! Cars were invariably dark blue and, prior to 1910, a shade of Brewster green. But the need to increase output to cope with demand led to the use of a quick-drying paint and black Japan enamel provided the answer, although the subsequent colour varnish and finishing coats required that the bodies be stored for a further twenty-four hours before they could be united with the chassis.

Above all, the arrival of mass production brought a dramatic reduction in prices. Burgeoning demand had already cut the T's introductory price of $850 to $600

Unpainted bodies arriving at Highland Park in late 1913. These were built by an outside contractor and then completed by Ford. Ironically the Model T made a major contribution to the demise of horsepower.

Frank Kulick at the wheel of his Model T Ford-based racer on the frozen Lake St Clair in the winter of 1912. It averaged 107.8 mph (173.48 km/h) but the engine was produced by the Ford experimental department! By this time it was known as 999 II in memory of Henry Ford's famous racer of 1903 vintage.

(£123) in 1913. In the following year came a further reduction, to $550 (£113), then to $490 (£100) in 1915, and by 1918 the price was down to $360 (£74). Despite rising, briefly, to $575 (£114) in 1920, it continued to tumble as output soared, hitting a low in 1925–6 when just $260 (£61) would buy a two-seater Runabout.

Over the years, countless modifications were effected to the car although the Tin Lizzie still retained the essence of the 1908 original. The bodies had originally been made of wood but this was replaced in 1911 by steel. The 1917 model year marked the end of the T's handsome brass radiator: from then on it shared the black body colour. It would not be until the 1926 season that a choice of colours was again reintroduced and the plated radiator reappeared.

The United States entered the First World War in 1917. By then the Model T had already proved its worth (see page 19). When the Armistice was signed in November 1918 the car had been in production for ten years.

Henry Ford's fame had spread by then far beyond his native America and he emerged as the most famous industrialist in the world. The millionth Ford – it could be nothing else but a Model T – had been built on 10th December 1915. Output had continued to rise and in 1918 Ford manufactured a record 642,750 cars. With a total of 1,275,324 automobiles produced worldwide that year, this represented an astounding 50.4 per cent of global car output, and demand showed no sign of abating. Could the T go on for ever?

'The Universal Car'

In 1913, Glen Buck, a go-getting Chicago advertising agent, took over the editorship of the corporate *Ford Times* established in April 1908, the same year the Model T was introduced. Buck had been responsible, in 1912, for the design of a corporate motif, a winged pyramidal device that obliquely echoed the T's much vaunted three-point suspension. The motif incorporated the unequivocal legend: 'Ford The Universal Car', which reflected the fact that the Model T had already established a strong European footing. That

The winged pyramid corporate motif, introduced in 1912 and used until the early 1920s.

year it became Britain's top-selling car, and after the war its influence would extend throughout the world.

However, Ford's first foreign assembly operation had been established in Canada in 1905 and thus predated the T. This branch, founded in the previous year, was based in Walkerville, Ontario, just across the Detroit River. Production began in 1908, followed in 1913 by engine manufacture, and some five plants were subsequently established throughout the country. Canada also exported its products, some in right-hand-drive form, throughout the British Empire but with the exception of Britain itself.

Fords had been imported there since the winter of 1903–4, and a London branch, following American practice, was set up in 1909, headed by the able Percival Perry, who had been associated with the make since its arrival in Britain. His commitment was further underpinned when he established a rapport with Henry Ford during a

'The Universal Car' in a British outlet in 1919, a boom year in which the five-seater Touring Car in the centre sold for £220. The Sedan behind it was considerably more expensive at £375. Only left-hand-drive cars were available at this time.

14

Percival Lea Dewhurst Perry (1878–1956), whose involvement with Ford's British operations began in 1904 and continued, apart from a six-year break in the 1920s, until he retired as chairman in 1948. He was knighted in 1918 and elevated to the peerage in 1938.

visit he made to Detroit in 1906. Except for the period 1922–8, Perry was to continue to direct the company's British operations until 1948.

Right-hand-drive Model Ts were received in crated form by the London-based agency. But Ford trusted Perry, and the T's British sales (1023 cars sold in two years) made the company decide to manufacture the model in Britain, the first such operation outside North America. The Ford Motor Company (England) Ltd was accordingly incorporated on 8th March 1911. Two months later, in May, Henry Alexander, who had held the Ford agency in Edinburgh since 1906, hit the headlines when he reached the summit of Ben Nevis at the wheel of a Model T. The feat received worldwide publicity. Perry once again proved his worth and he had also found a factory in which to produce the British-built Ford. It had hitherto been used for the production of Manchester tramcars on the western outskirts of that city at Trafford Park, which was Britain's first industrial estate. Conveniently close to the Manchester Ship Canal, it thus met the corporate requirement of having access to navigable water, so that parts and raw materials could be shipped in and cars driven out.

Henry Alexander in a Model T in the process of conquering the 4406 feet (1343 metre) Ben Nevis, the highest mountain in the British Isles, in May 1911.

Above: *Model T chassis at Trafford Park, prior to having their bodies fitted. The date is 1913.*

Left: *A 1913 Trafford Park Model T in dark green with a Scott Brothers body photographed soon after its completion.*

Using parts imported from the United States, the first British-built Ford was assembled on 23rd October 1911. Perry's intention, however, was to produce as much as possible locally. This was eventually achieved and, by the mid 1920s, about 90 per cent of the Model T was being made within the British Isles. Initially bodies were supplied by the nearby Scott Brothers but, when that company was unable to cope with demand, Ford absorbed the business. Trafford Park produced radiators and wings although the chassis and engine/transmissions were shipped from the United States. This continued until 1921, when Ford's Cork plant began to supply these major mechanicals, and chassis production was allocated to Joseph Sankey of Hadley, Shropshire.

In 1912, Ford England's first full year, 3081 examples of the value-for-money

The author in 1980, having survived the delights of Henry Ford's epicyclic transmission, at the wheel of a 1913 tourer loaned to the Ford Motor Company.

Right: *Part of the exterior of Ford's Trafford Park factory in 1914. Used by the company between 1911 and 1931, it was initially capable of producing only fifteen thousand chassis a year, but it was reorganised to manufacture thirty thousand.*

The Trafford Park body shop in 1914. Originally coachwork was supplied by the nearby Scott Brothers company which was absorbed by Ford in July 1913.

Model T were sold on the British market, and it thus became the country's best-selling car. It remained so until 1923.

In the United States the Highland Park moving-track assembly line was in place by April 1914 and that month Charles Sorensen visited Trafford Park to assist with the installation of the concept in Britain. Manchester-built Model Ts were being produced this way by September and the plant became not only Britain's but also Europe's most productive car factory. In 1914 Britons bought no fewer than 8352 Fords.

But 1914 also saw the outbreak of the First World War and Ford England was well placed to maintain Model T production, which continued throughout hostilities. Some thirty thousand vehicles were supplied to the British government, many being

A Manchester-built Model T outside Ford's London showrooms at 55–59 Shaftesbury Avenue in 1914. The use of these premises predated the formation of Ford England in 1911, as they opened in October 1909.

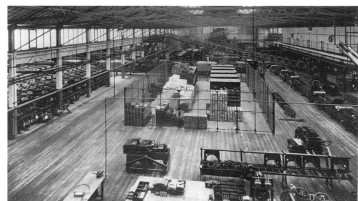

Britain's first moving-track assembly line was operational at the Manchester factory from 1914. Note the gravity-fed wheel chute. This photograph was taken in 1915.

The Model T was designed to carry five adults, and this Manchester-built Tourer of 1915 has a full load. The driver's door is false. This three-door body was available until c.1918.

Trafford Park also produced its cars in chassis form for bodying by specialist coachbuilders. This car dates from c.1914. That year, a hundred chassis were so supplied.

Dr R. Latimer Greene of Stratford-upon-Avon, Warwickshire, in August 1915 with his Runabout, the first of a succession of Model Ts that he owned. His grandson, John Moulton, still recalls him jacking up the rear wheel to start it on cold mornings! The house in the background was Dr Latimer Greene's surgery and survives, almost unchanged, as council offices.

used for transporting troops and as field ambulances. The Ford's versatility and durable qualities proved their worth not only on the Western Front but also in the Middle East. There the legendary Lawrence of Arabia recognised that there were only two vehicles capable of withstanding the rigours of the Mesopotamian desert: one was the Rolls-Royce Silver Ghost and the other was Ford's ubiquitous, spidery, but indestructible Model T.

Most other British domestic car production had ceased in 1916 so Ford, with its uninterrupted output, was well placed to benefit from the short-lived boom that followed the Armistice. In a fifteen-month period in 1919–20, its English branch sold an astounding 46,362 Model T cars, trucks and vans. This figure represented the high point of its Manchester operation and would not be bettered until 1935, by

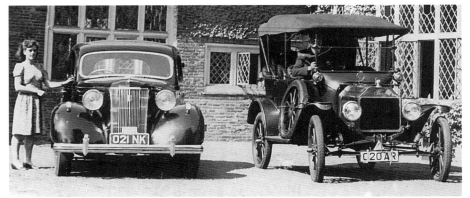

A 1915 Model T in company with a later Ford product, the Dagenham-built V8 Pilot produced between 1947 and 1951.

which time Ford had removed to Dagenham, Essex.

From then on Model T car sales went into decline. The first blow came in 1921 when the government introduced the 'horsepower tax', a protectionist measure aimed at penalising American-designed cars. With a formula related to an engine's bore, the Ford was rated at 22 hp whereas the native Morris Cowley was 11.9 hp. These cost their respective owners £22 and £12 a year to tax, and this was one reason why the British car overtook Ford's hitherto pre-eminent position in 1924. (The tax did not apply to the T's commercial vehicle derivatives, which outsold the cars from 1924. See page 27.) Further uncertainties were caused by Percival Perry falling out with Henry Ford and resigning from the company in 1922. Also, in an attempt at rationalisation, Detroit insisted that only left-hand-drive cars be produced in 1919–23, and this underlined the T's transatlantic origins.

In 1917, Ford had established a branch in Cork on a site that fronted the river Lee. Conceived as a factory for the mechanically unrelated Fordson tractor, Model T assembly began there in 1921 because Cork had been chosen for the site of the first Ford foundry to be established in the Old World. It was thus able to supply Manchester with engines, transmissions and machined parts, with complete cars

A 1920 Ford. Note the electric headlamps, which were introduced in 1915. It is pictured with a prototype caravan by Bertram Hutchings of Winchester, Hampshire, a firm that later marketed the Winchester as 'The Rolls-Royce of Caravans'.

The two hundred and fifty thousandth Manchester-built Ford was completed on 17th April 1925. The Union Jack flags underlined that the overwhelming majority of components were British-made. But whilst the Model T now had a plated radiator, it still lacked front-wheel brakes.

following in 1923. When the Irish Free State came into being in 1922, these components became subject to a 22 $^2/_9$ per cent import duty, a move which further added to the cost of the Model T.

It was this unsatisfactory state of affairs that led Ford to look for a fresh factory site: in 1924 it bought 295 acres (120 hectares) of Essex marshland at Dagenham, and

The celebratory British Ford on display. As can be seen, Ford England went to great lengths to distance itself from its United States origins. These cars were originally lower than their American counterparts on account of a drop-frame chassis, introduced in 1924, and then copied by Detroit!

A line-up of Fords outside a British dealer's showroom in 1927, the last year of production. The T Tourer was still remarkably good value at £125 – £23 cheaper than the comparable Morris Cowley, which retailed for £148. But the Ford still cost £22 a year to tax.

This unregistered Model T was photographed in 1978 in the showrooms of C. E. M. Day of Swansea, South Wales, still for sale, and having covered only 124 miles (200 km). Built on 4th July 1926, it was bought by a sub-dealer, from whom Mr Day acquired it in 1948.

A German-built Model T which headed a procession of Fords from the company's Berlin factory to a new plant located in the city of Cologne on the Rhine in 1931. The message on the side of the car reads: 'To our new home'.

in 1931 it opened its new plant there.

Ford had exported Model Ts to France from its 1908 inception but assembly did not begin there until during the First World War in 1916, when a factory was hurriedly established at Bordeaux. After the war, a new, larger facility was opened in 1926 on the river Seine in the Paris suburb of Asnières. In 1919, Model Ts had begun to leave a plant in Copenhagen; this Danish facility was followed in 1920 by a Spanish operation at Cadiz, and two years later a Ford factory was built in Hoboken, Belgium, near to the port of Antwerp. Germany had to wait until 1926, when Ford's Berlin branch, established in a former riverside warehouse at Plotzensee, came on stream. South African assembly began in 1924 and Australian in the following year. In Asia, it started in Malaya in 1922, Japan in 1925 and India in 1926. Latin America had its first Ford factory in Argentina in 1916; Uruguay followed in 1920, Chile in 1924 and Mexico in 1925. With such world-wide presences, Ford's 'Universal Car' was precisely that.

There was not a garage in inter-war America unfamiliar with the Model T's mechanicals. Note how the engine/trans-mission is removable as a single unit.

The world on wheels

The 1920s were Henry Ford's decade as Model T output continued to soar. No less than one million cars and trucks were produced in 1922, a year in which company profits rose to a record $119 million (£26 million), and, incredibly, in 1923 output doubled again to two million. But thereafter the rapidly ageing Tin Lizzie settled into a gentle decline and production ceased in 1927.

Although outwardly the all-black Fords appeared much the same as their pre-war counterparts, some refinements had been introduced. From 1919, the T was given a battery and an electric starter; it became a standard fitment on the more expensive closed versions and, by mid 1919, an option on the T Tourer. New body styles arrived with the Fordor Sedan, a name that echoed its allocation of doors, appearing for the 1923 season, followed for 1924 by its Tudor stablemate.

Another milestone was passed on 24th June 1924 when the ten millionth Ford, a T of course, was manufactured. This also marked the peak of Highland Park's influence: no less than 68,285 people were employed there that year, after which its importance slowly waned, having been eclipsed from 1925 onwards by a new massive factory complex that Ford was building on the banks of Detroit's Rouge River.

This move had been prompted by a lack of space for expansion at the factory that had served the company so well since 1910. So in 1915, a mere three years after its completion, Ford bought some 2000 acres (814 hectares) of land, mostly to the east of the Rouge where it entered the Detroit River. There, from 1918, it began the con-struction of the largest industrial concentration the world had ever seen, a process that continued until 1937.

Such was the efficiency of the Rouge plant that, in 1923, Ford was able to claim that what had been iron on a Monday would, two and a half days later, be powering a complete car. The sequence was as follows: on Monday at 8 a.m., ore from Ford's own mine at Michigamme, Ohio, would be unloaded to feed the massive blast furnaces. On Tuesday at 12.10 a.m, sixteen hours later, the ore had been reduced to foundry iron and then to pig iron. At 4.10 p.m. on the same day, it would be cast into cylinder blocks, which were then machined and assembled. It took just ninety-seven minutes to build a Model T engine. Power units were then loaded aboard special trains, which ran day and night, to a branch for assembly. This was completed by 8 a.m. on Wednesday. At 12 noon the dealer would have paid for the car and taken delivery of it. The conversion of raw materials into cash had taken just thirty-three

A 1920 Centerdoor Sedan, introduced for 1915 and available until mid 1923, when it was replaced by the Tudor Sedan. It was possible to squeeze in five travellers. The detachable wheel rims arrived as an optional fitment on the closed Ts in 1919.

Left: *October 1924: this style of Fordor Sedan was produced between the end of 1923 and 1925. The nickel door handles represented one of the few pieces of brightwork on the car.*

Below: *A 1926 season Runabout, which sold for the all-time low price of $260 (£61)! This is a pre-production example as it is fitted with small rear brake drums. These were increased to 11 inches (279 mm) diameter for the 1926 model year.*

hours with transportation and handling accounting for fifteen.

In August 1925, the Model T was given a facelift which was the first restyling since 1917. Although initially offered in black, the Coupé and Fordor were available in dark green and the Fordor Sedan in dark maroon. There was a reversion to a plated radiator shell, although nickel replaced the brass discontinued in 1916. Standardised on the closed Model Ts, it was also an optional fitment on the Tourers. Later, in 1926, colour was introduced to the open cars. The T's wooden wheels were already looking dated and wire wheels were offered as an option from January 1926, and from 1927 many of Ford's branches were fitting them as standard on the closed cars.

Despite this, the T was nearing the end of the road, and becoming less and less competitive in the face of sure-footed opposition from General Motors' Chevrolet make. Initially, an increasingly obdurate Henry Ford held out against the entreaties of his staff to discontinue the car, but on 26th May 1927 the news broke across the United States that the Model T was to be replaced.

On the following day, 27th May, he drove the fifteen millionth car off the Highland Park assembly line and the much publicised 'last car', number 15,007,033, was produced on 31st May. However, over the summer the United States built a further 484,781 Ts, which brought the total to 15,491,814. To this have to be added another 747,748 made by Ford Canada and 301,980 made by Trafford Park, the final example being built there on 19th August 1927. The last European T was produced on 31st December, when Cork completed a run of 10,341 cars destined for the Irish market.

Left: *Ford's huge Rouge River complex in about 1928. The company's ore-carrying ships are in the right foreground with storage bins to their left. Dominating the site are the tall chimneys of the power station with blast furnaces and foundries to the left.*

Below: *The rolling mill at Rouge River was capable of handling between fifteen and twenty thousand tons of steel a month. Its function was to roll steel into bars for use on the Model T car and TT Truck.*

This makes a grand total of about 16.5 million Models Ts built worldwide between 1908 and 1927.

Ford America continued to produce replacement engines and output was maintained to a maximum of twelve thousand a month until 1931, thereafter dropping sharply to one hundred. Their manufacture continued until 4th August 1941, fourteen years after the model had ceased production.

The T's much heralded replacement, the Rouge-built Model A, was announced on 1st December 1927 and although it was to sell well (some 5.02 million would be built) it lacked that spark of genius that had made the Model T so special. In 1931, a now six-cylinder-powered Chevrolet overtook Ford as America's best-selling car maker and its General Motors parent, having got in front, stayed there.

In the current age of soaring development costs, the world car is commonplace but it is sobering to reflect that today's motor manufacturers are following in the Model T Ford's wheel tracks that first turned way back in 1908.

Stan Laurel chauffeurs Oliver Hardy in a special articulated Model T in the twenty-minute Hal Roach comedy 'County Hospital', released in 1932.

This 1914 car chassis was typical of many that were fitted with an overlarge body. The removal van belonged to a contractor based in St Leonards-on-Sea, Sussex.

Commercially speaking

From the very outset, the Model T's tough, reliable pedigree lent itself to a host of uses other than for transporting passengers. Farmers regularly overloaded it and harnessed its power to drive their machinery whilst such companies as Eros and Ajax even offered them tractor conversion kits. The T also formed the basis of the Delivery Car that Ford America offered in 1912. It did not sell well: a mere 1845 examples were produced that season and when the total dropped to 513 in 1913 it was discontinued.

Ford England's sales were much more buoyant and from 1921 commercial vehicle sales were not damaged, as the car had been, by the arrival of the horsepower tax. Unlike the private vehicle tax, the commercial levy was not based on an engine's bore but a vehicle's weight, which benefited the lightweight T.

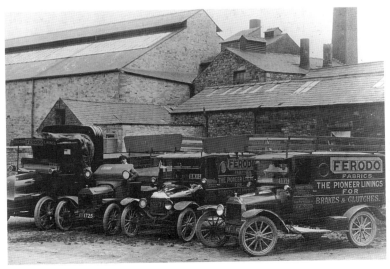

The fleet of the clutch manufacturer Ferodo in 1915. A Model T works-bodied Delivery Van is on the right with further variants on the Ford theme to the left.

The Model T-based Hucks starter, created in 1915 by Captain Benny Hucks, test pilot for the Airco company of Hendon. A chain and sprocket mechanism transferred power from the T's epicyclic transmission and, until the arrival of inertia and electric starting methods in the 1930s, was the only way to start large aero engines. The aeroplane is a Bristol fighter.

In 1912 Trafford Park began to offer its Delivery Van, which was capable of carrying loads of up to 7 hundredweight (356 kg) and was destined to be the most popular line in what was to grow into a Model T-based commercial vehicle range. By the time that production ceased in 1927, a total of 59,091 examples had been built and, from 1924, more were sold than Model T cars. The vans' reliability and low cost proved an irresistible combination to customers, whether large companies or one-man bakery or confectionery businesses. The irrevocable switch from horsepower to the internal combustion engine often came with the purchase of Henry Ford's Model T-based van, which soon dominated the market.

A further variant came when the First World War began in 1914 and the carnage of the Western Front produced a demand for ambulances. Ford France accordingly converted ten Manchester-supplied Ts with makeshift bodies. Trafford Park began production in 1915, and a total of 2645 Model T ambulances were built between then and 1919, a total which includes a singleton in 1920.

The car-derived van chassis were also purchased by firms and individuals and then bodied by coachbuilders to their requirements. The resulting vehicles tended

Model T ambulances bodied by J. Blake & Co of Liverpool, completed in 1915. The firm had also been appointed a Ford dealer in 1910.

to be overbodied and, in consequence, overloaded. An answer to this problem was to extend the T's chassis, and a number of companies offered conversions. One of the best known was BAICO (the British American Import Company), dating from 1914, which operated from premises in London's Fulham Road. Costing £92, with 'no skilled labour needed to make the change', it entailed lengthening the Ford's frame whilst retaining the original rear axle. The back wheels were removed and replaced by sprockets which then drove, by chains, a strengthened secondary axle with half-elliptic spring suspension. The payload was accordingly trebled, to one ton (1016 kg). In addition, BAICO bodied standard Model T frames as well as their extended ones, and Ford England gave the conversion its approval.

It was not until the beginning of 1918 that Ford in the United States responded to its customers' demands for a stronger vehicle by introducing a more robust commercial version of the Model T. This truck, with a one-ton payload, carried the TT designation. Whilst its engine/gearbox was essentially the same as that used in the car, it had a new, more robust and elongated chassis with a 10 foot 4 inch (3150 mm) wheelbase which was 2 feet (610 mm) longer. It retained the familiar rear transverse-leaf spring suspension but the back axle was new, being a stronger and more efficient overhead worm-drive unit. The wooden artillery wheels were shod with solid rear tyres although from 1919 the TT was offered with the option of smaller diameter pneumatics.

Until 1924, Detroit offered the TT only in chassis form. But in January came the C cab, so called because of the shape of its glassless apertures, and April saw the arrival of an all-steel cab. Over a million TTs were built during a ten-year manufacturing life.

British production of the Truck also began in 1918 and, like the van, the TT

Left: *Although this bus is based on a TT chassis of c.1923, it appears to be a trifle overbodied. It was built by coachbuilders and Ford dealers G. Davidson & Sons of Whitley Bay, Northumberland.*

Below: *A TT Truck (right) outside Davidson's premises. It was well priced at £132 and the annual tax was £16 rather than the car's £22. It is keeping company with a Fordson tractor built at the Rouge plant in Detroit and also by Ford's Irish branch at Cork.*

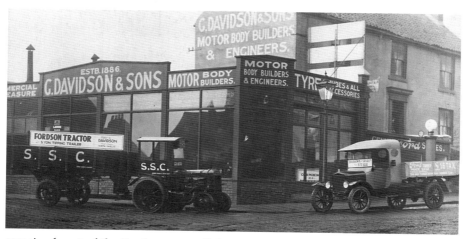

remained part of the Ford range until the Model T car ceased manufacture in 1927. The mainstream version was the factory-built Truck and a respectable 37,556 examples were made. The Ton Van was also available between 1921 and 1927, and 11,307 were sold. However, the TT chassis that was then bodied by a coachbuilder of the customer's own choice was still much more popular, with 56,301 leaving Trafford Park over the same period.

The TT was offered with a variety of bodies. It proved popular with charabanc and coach operators, formed the basis of horse boxes and furniture vans whilst both BP and Pratts motor spirit used them as tankers for petrol deliveries. The Post Office was an important and influential customer and, between 1921 and 1926, bought over one thousand Ford vans, both the TT and its 7 hundredweight predecessor.

The arrival of the TT rendered the BAICO conversion obsolete but the enterprising company responded by applying its ingenuity to the new model. It produced the Extendatonna, with a lengthened frame in which the existing axle was relocated,

Above: *A 1926 TT with works Truck body. Such vehicles continued to serve their owners reliably until the Second World War.*

Right: *The Model T immortalised on a stamp in the Post Office's Great British Motor Cars series issued in October 1982. It is depicted with a Ford Escort, a best-selling car in Britain although corporate hopes of it being a true world car, like the Model T, were never realised.*

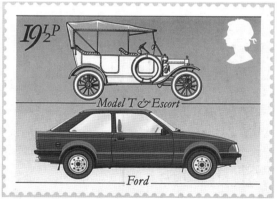

requiring an extended torque tube, and, once again, with rear half-elliptic springs. This gave a 30 hundredweight (1512 kg) capacity. It also produced the top-of-the-range Supertonna with a 2.5 ton (2540 kg) load limit. Available with a variety of wheelbases, it reverted to the chain drive of the original. Whilst the customary two-speed epicyclic gearbox was retained, a conventional three-speed unit was positioned behind it.

When van and TT production ceased at Trafford Park in 1927 the T-based models were replaced by two Model A-related designs, so laying firm foundations for Ford commercial vehicle lines that survive to this day.

Further reading

The quality of material on the Ford company and the Model T is particularly good; although most of the titles listed below are out of print they are not difficult to find in specialist bookshops and at autojumbles.

Autocar Special. *Picture a Ford*. IPC Business Press, 1980.
Clymer, Floyd. *Henry's Wonderful Model T*. McGraw-Hill, 1955.
McCalley, Bruce W. *Model T Ford: The Car That Changed the World*. Krause Publications, 1994.
Nevins, Allan, and Hill, Frank Ernest. *Ford: The Times, The Man, The Company*. Charles Scribner's Sons, 1954.
Nevins, Allan, and Hill, Frank Ernest. *Ford: Expansion and Challenge 1915–1933*. Charles Scribner's Sons, 1957.
Riley, Martin, Lilleker, Bruce, and Tuckett, Neil. *The English Model T Ford*. Model T Ford Register of Great Britain, 2008.
Sorensen, Charles W., with Samuel T. Williamson. *Forty Years with Ford*. Jonathan Cape, 1957.
Stern, Philip Van Doren. *Tin Lizzie: The Story of the Fabulous Model T Ford*. Simon & Schuster, 1955.
Wilkins, Mira, and Hill, Frank Ernest. *American Business Abroad: Ford on Six Continents*. Wayne State University Press, 1964.

Places to visit

The world's finest collection of Ford cars, company history and Americana is at Greenfield Village and the Henry Ford Museum at 20900 Oakwood Boulevard, Dearborn, Michigan 48121, USA. In Britain, the Ford Motor Company has three Model Ts on display at its Dagenham-based Ford Heritage Centre. Viewing is part of a factory tour and details can be obtained from Room 3/001, Thames Avenue, Dagenham, Essex RM9 6SA. Model Ts can also be seen at the following museums but it is always advisable to check before making a journey.

Atwell-Wilson Motor Museum, Downside, Stockley Lane, Calne, Wiltshire SN11 0NF. Telephone: 01249 813119. Website: www.atwellwilson.org.uk
Lakeland Motor Museum, Holker Hall and Gardens, Cark-in-Cartmel, Grange-over-Sands, South Lakeland, Cumbria LA11 7PL. Telephone: 015395 58509. Website: www.lakelandmotormuseum.co.uk
Llangollen Motor Museum, Pentre Fellin, Llangollen LL20 8EE. Telephone: 01978 860324. Website: www.llangollenmotormuseum.co.uk
Museum of British Road Transport, Hales Street, Coventry CV1 1PN. Telephone: 024 7263 4270. Website: www.transport-museum.com
National Motor Museum, Beaulieu, Hampshire SO42 7ZN. Telephone: 01590 612345. Website: www.beaulieu.co.uk
Shuttleworth Collection, Old Warden Aerodrome, Biggleswade, Bedfordshire SG18 9EP. Telephone: 01767 627288. Website: www.shuttleworth.org

Examples of this famous Ford can often be seen at veteran and vintage car rallies. The British club that caters for the T is *The Model T Register of Great Britain*; the membership secretary is Mrs Julia M. Armer, 195 Bradford Road, Riddlesden, Keighley, West Yorkshire BD20 5JR. Many countries have their clubs although, inevitably, the United States is best represented. The Model T Club of America's address is PO Box 126, , Centerville, Illinois 47330-0126, USA.

This 1920 Model T Delivery Van spent much of its life on the streets of Blackpool and is on display at the Lakeland Motor Museum at Cark-in-Cartmel, Cumbria. A 1927 Ford converted as a shooting brake can also be seen there.